Too Busy?

Saying No Without Guilt

Alice Fryling

InterVarsity Press
P.O. Box 1400, Downers Grove, IL 60515-1426
World Wide Web: www.ivpress.com
E-mail: mail@ivpress.com

©2002 by Alice Fryling

All rights reserved. No part of this book may be reproduced in any form without written permission from InterVarsity Press.

InterVarsity Press® is the book-publishing division of InterVarsity Christian Fellowship/USA®, a student movement active on campus at hundreds of universities, colleges and schools of nursing in the United States of America, and a member movement of the International Fellowship of Evangelical Students. For information about local and regional activities, write Public Relations Dept., InterVarsity Christian Fellowship/ USA, 6400 Schroeder Rd., P.O. Box 7895, Madison, WI 53707-7895, or visit the IVCF website at <www.ivcf.org>.

All Scripture quotations, unless otherwise indicated, are taken from the Holy Bible, New International Version®. NIV®. Copyright ©1973, 1978, 1984 by International Bible Society. Used by permission of Zondervan Publishing House. All rights reserved.

ISBN 0-87784-049-0

Printed in the United States of America ∞

P	13	12	11	10	9	8	7	6	5	4	3	2	1
Y	12	11	10	09	08	07	06	05	04	03	02			

*To my brother-in-law, Dr. John Stanford
(Thank you, John!)*

*Come to me, all you who are weary and burdened,
and I will give you rest.*
JESUS OF NAZARETH

As I look at these familiar words of Jesus, I know that I qualify: I am weary and burdened. I wouldn't use those exact words; in fact, I probably wouldn't admit it at all. If the phone rings and I hear a friend ask, "Hi, how are you?" I might be tempted to say, "Oh fine—busy but fine." I certainly would *not* say, "I am weary and burdened"!

But I know it is to me that Jesus speaks. And not only to me: most of us fill our days with as much as possible, accomplishing all we can. We produce to our limits and beyond. We pack our days and nights full of good things—our job, our family, church activities, community service, sports and entertainment. And at the end of these full days, we are often weary.

But to do less, to be less productive, does not seem like an option. We all know that opportunity knocks but once; what if we are sitting down when opportunity comes by? What if we miss our one chance?

To those of us who struggle with this perspective, the actions of Jesus, as recorded by the Gospel writer Mark, seem strange indeed. Jesus had gotten people's attention through his teaching and healing. On one occasion "the whole town gathered at the door" where he was staying (Mark 1:21-39)—a great opportunity for Jesus to share the love of God. The next morning, according to Mark, Jesus got up and left. How could he walk out on such an opportunity? How could he leave all those people waiting to be healed, to be taught, to be touched by God? How *could* you, Jesus?

I would not have left. I would have said, "These

people need me," or "God needs me to reach these people." I would not have been so foolish as to leave when I was being sought after. I am a person who recognizes the opportunity to serve. I do not run away.

But if I am honest enough to say I would not have done what Jesus did, then I need to ask myself a very serious question: Am I saying "Yes" when Jesus would say "No"? Christian teaching often asks, "Are you willing to go wherever God sends you?" But what if the question is "Are you willing not to go where God does not send you?" That may be a harder question to answer.

After all, aren't Christians supposed to serve? Aren't we supposed to do good works for the sake of the kingdom of God? The answer to both these questions is, of course, yes. But as we look at our overbooked schedules and high levels of stress and fatigue, to say nothing of the dryness in our souls, we have to ask if it is not true that something has gone awry.

Can you picture Jesus rushing down the street, talking on his cell phone, bumping shoulders as he weaves through the crowd to hurry to his afternoon meeting? Or can you imagine Jesus packing his life with fitness programs, concerts and sporting events? Even if Jesus were living on earth in the twenty-first century, I do not think he would be living as many of us are. No, Jesus' life reflected a confidence centered in his Father, who guided his interactions and activities in such a way that Jesus could avoid being rushed, could feel free not to meet every opportunity, and could promise that if we follow him, we will have peace.

Jesus had time to notice people in need, talk to people with questions and interact with people in their ordinary lives. But he did not meet every need, he did not answer every question, and he did not embrace every opportunity. When Jesus taught in the synagogue, he reminded the people that God has focused plans.

> There were many widows in Israel in Elijah's time. . . . Yet Elijah was not sent to any of them, but to a widow in Zarephath in the region of Sidon. And there were many in Israel with leprosy in the time of Elisha the prophet, yet not one of them was

cleansed—only Naaman the Syrian. (Luke 4:25-27)

Against the backdrop of his unhurried, intentional life, Jesus made this remarkable promise:

> Come to me, all you who are weary and burdened, and I will give you rest. Take my yoke upon you and learn from me, for I am gentle and humble in heart, and you will find rest for your souls. For my yoke is easy and my burden is light. (Matthew 11:28-30)

Centuries later, Jesus has not changed. He still invites us to come to him and find rest for our souls. By using the image of a yoke, Jesus acknowledges that rest for our souls includes work (animals were yoked together to pull heavy loads), but he promises that his work (his load) for us will not be heavy or burdensome.

Why then are Christians so often weary and burdened? Why are our souls far from rested? I believe we miss his rest because we reject his yoke in favor of the stressful yokes of our society and because we fail to emulate his gentleness and humility.

The Yoke of Our Society

Jesus' yoke is easy, his burden light, but we have chosen to carry idols that are "burdensome" (Isaiah 46:1). Our idols have remote controls, electronic memories and digital readouts. We look to them to control our lives so that we can get more, do more and be more. Technology has given us so much, from instant communication with our friends to unprecedented speed in our work, that we live with the illusion that we have ready access to all we need. Set against our efforts to squeeze the most out of our lives, Jesus' promise to give us rest may sound outdated and irrelevant. As the Israelites were with their idols, so we may be with ours: "The good news came to them; but the message which they heard did not benefit them, because it did not meet with faith in the hearers" (Hebrews 4:2 NRSV).

Laptops, palm display units and cell phones promise an easier life, but in reality they deliver increased stress and pressure. Physicians and psychologists tell us that our bodies are not designed for the constant input of our technological age, for being always "on." We need "down" times when our adrenaline can subside, when we can muse and dream and be restored. But the God-given rhythms of day and night, work and rest, have been usurped by technological potential. I live in a city where lights are on all night and the expressways see traffic at 2 a.m. The opportunities for activity in my city never, ever cease.

Add to this pace the high value placed on personal potential, and we have a recipe for anxiety and stress. American culture teaches, "You can do anything you want to do." The more times we say yes, the more affirmation we get—the busier, the better. I heard one person speak admiringly of another: "She couldn't be busier." I heard a mother praise her son: "He is a wonderful boy—so driven." A Christian executive pushes employees: "If we work at this, we can be a multimillion-dollar company in five years." We live under the shadow of busyness and drivenness.

The church, while not embracing all that society teaches, is understandably influenced by this emphasis on potential. We want to make our church programs more attractive, more user-friendly, more seeker-sensitive, so we push ourselves to be proactive and available. Our motivation may be very good, but as we focus on making our presentation of the gospel attractive and relevant, we can lose sight of Jesus. With so many items on our agenda, it may seem like a waste of time to stop long enough to be quiet and prayerful. With programs to run, properties to care for and budgets to accommodate, we just do not have time to deepen our relationship with God.

Jesus is not a project manager trying to maximize the potential of his employees. And he is not a dictator or a slave-driver. According to biblical imagery, he is our lover. The church is the bride of Christ (Revelation 21:2). Through our convoluted, unbiblical thinking, however, we have gotten ourselves into a situation where the bride does not have time for the bridegroom.

We may wonder if Jesus' invitation to find rest for our souls is totally archaic. We shake our heads and say, "God only knows how we can live quiet lives in this day and age." The good news is that God does know! Jesus said, "Learn from me, for I am gentle and humble in heart." Even in the twenty-first century, Jesus' gentleness speaks to that part of our being that is shrouded in self-doubt and low self-esteem, and his humility speaks to that part of us that is puffed up and egocentric.

The Gentleness of Jesus

My husband jokes, "We tell people 'Come to Jesus and he will meet all your needs.' They come to Jesus and find out what their needs are: they need to do this and they need to do that!" The joke would be funnier if it weren't so true. Where did we get the idea that being a good Christian means "do and do, do and do" (Isaiah 28:10)?

Some of us learned as children that whatever we did was not good enough, so we do and do in the hopes that one of those do's will prove our worth. Others of us learned a theology that says salvation may be by grace, but discipleship means burning out for Jesus—though in fact it was said of Jesus, "A bruised reed he will not break, / and a smoldering wick he will not snuff out" (Matthew 12:20).

Still others feel so overwhelmed by the world's

problems that instead of "do-do-do" they suffer from "can't-can't-can't." They are immobilized by the magnitude of the problems of world hunger, global warming and the AIDS epidemic. Underneath their withdrawal lurks despair: they could never do enough even if they tried.

To all these people Jesus says, "Come to me." Eugene Peterson translates Jesus' promise of rest this way: "Learn the unforced rhythms of grace. I won't lay anything heavy or ill-fitting on you" (Matthew 11:29 The Message). Jesus does not intend for us to carry the heavy burden of ill-fitting good works. If we were to join him at the dinner table, where he did much of his teaching during his life on earth, he might remind us that we do not need to do everything, that burnout is not his idea of obedience and that by God's grace even a little bit goes a long way. He might tell us about a little boy who offered a small lunch to feed thousands (John 6:5-13). Or he might remind us of the widow who gave "all she had to live on"—two small copper coins (Luke 21:4). When we feel that we have given all we can give, perhaps Jesus whispers, "It is enough." By his grace, our small "seeds" may grow into mustard trees (Matthew 13:31-32).

Craig Barnes, in his book *Sacred Thirst,* suggests that "the real question for every disciple of Jesus Christ is not, am I effective?—but, do I believe that Jesus Christ is effective?"[1] This does not mean that we should be passive or lazy; rather, the focus for our activity must be Jesus, the only one who can really do all that we wish we could do. We can assume that God is at work and that we are only participants in the work he is already doing.

In fact, as we take on Jesus' yoke, we find that the work we are yoked to do has been custom-made for us. The apostle Paul wrote, "We are God's workmanship, created in Christ Jesus to do good works, which God prepared in advance for us to do" (Ephesians 2:10). In my own experience, doing the works that he has prepared for me to do, while not always easy, always brings a sense of inner freedom, joy and growing confidence. If, for days at a time, I am unable to tune in to God's gentleness or to experience his peace, the distress in my soul may be a signal that I am doing works he has not designed for me.

The Humility of Jesus

Jesus is gentle with us when we are weary and burdened, but he is also humble. Sometimes our busyness and weariness grow out of self-doubt, but other times our pride gets us into trouble. In our pride we may push ourselves beyond our limits in ways that bring to mind Adam and Eve, our ancestors from the Garden of Eden.

Adam and Eve were created with jobs to *do*—to name the animals, care for the plants, and enjoy each other and their environment. But they thought they knew better than their Creator. They reached beyond the limits God had given them, wanting to eat of *every* tree in the Garden of Eden—even the one explicitly prohibited by God (Genesis 1—3).

We follow in their footsteps. We want what God has given us and more. We want to impress ourselves and others with all we do and all we can produce. We take God-given gifts, push them beyond their limits and make them sources of pride. It makes us feel good to be needed, to be useful. Such compulsive desires are unhealthy for our society at large; they are devastating when pursued in the name of God.

If we are honest, we must admit that much of what we do in God's name is motivated by our desire to look good. Our lips say that we want to honor God, but the truth may be that we want to show off our gifts or look important to others. I shudder to think of the prayer meetings I have attended where we prayed, "Lord, let us have the best meeting yet, so we can give glory to you." I fear our prayers are corrupted by pride to the point that, whatever words we speak, our hearts are actually praying, "Not thy will but mine be done."

God have mercy on us when we pray like that. Help us, Jesus, to come to you and to learn humility.

A Reorientation in Our Thinking

Humility requires not only honesty but a radical change in the way we think. Pride claims to always know the right thing to do. Humility takes away pride's confidence.

Consider Peter, who on several occasions thought he knew better than Jesus. When Jesus predicted his own death, Peter said, "Never, Lord! . . . This shall never happen to you!" (Matthew 16:22). When Jesus was arrested (Luke 22:47-51; John 18:3-11), Peter drew his sword to defend Jesus, cutting off the ear of Malchus, a servant with the arresting party. Jesus rebuked Peter and then healed the servant. (I wonder how often we do things that Jesus needs to undo!) Later, Peter experienced another reorientation of values when God told him to meet with Cornelius, a Gentile. Peter initially said, "Surely not, Lord! . . . I have never eaten anything impure or unclean" (Acts 10:14), but ultimately he met with Cornelius and witnessed the salvation of an entire household (Acts 10:44-47; 11:14).

Similarly, when God invites us to slow down, we may say, "No, Lord, I have never turned down a call to serve. I have always been a busy person." One day I made a list of my expectations for a given week. I added up the hours of preparation, carry-through and follow-up that all my expectations required. Then I listed the number of hours I had at my disposal. My expectations exceeded reality by almost ten hours! That meant that at least ten hours' worth of activity I was expecting to do was not God's will for me. What a sobering conclusion! I believe God is telling some of us that we need to let go of the value we place on service, availability and busyness, and take up the value God places on quietness, trust and peace.

This letting go is a very painful process of dying to self. We get instant affirmation from saying yes. We get personal stimulation from the idea of meeting a challenge, using our gifts or tapping into our creativity, and we avoid the unpleasantness of having to say no. But the gratification we have in saying yes may fade when we miss opportunities to be with those we love, or when we neglect our own sick souls. Our eager yes may be like go-now-pay-later vacation plans: when it comes time to pay, we wonder if going was really worth it.

Moving Toward Peace

I can remember crying out to a friend, "I *have* to do all I'm doing because the Bible says I am supposed to feed the poor, visit those in prison, and witness to my neighbors. But I'm just so tired!" My friend looked at me with the love of Jesus in his eyes and said, "I wish you could hear a voice from heaven saying, 'Alice, you don't have to do it *all*.'" Because of my friend's compassion I was able to hear God's Spirit in his words. That moment began a conversation with God which continues to this day. As I engage in this conversation, the Spirit whispers to my spirit in ways that move my soul toward peace.

God's Spirit continually reminds me not to believe the lies of busyness and drivenness. Instead of giving in to my knee-jerk reaction to say yes, sometimes I hear the Spirit whisper a divine no. He reminds me that he is a God who is not "served by human hands, as though he needed anything, since he himself gives to all mortals life and breath and all things" (Acts 17:25 NRSV). He even tells me,

> It is in vain that you rise up early
>   and go late to rest,
> eating the bread of anxious toil;
>   for he gives to his beloved sleep. (Ps 127:2 RSV)

This has been a major change in thinking for me. I used to think that doing the work of Jesus meant working hard at doing good works. While there is some truth in that, I have begun to see the truth of something Jesus said about himself. People asked him, "What must we do to do the works God requires?" His answer surprised me: "The work of God is this: to believe in the one he sent" (John 6:28, 29)—not to lead Bible studies, or be successful in business, studies or even relationships. These things may come as the result of belief, but the first work of God, Jesus said, is *to believe*. Amazing.

As I live with this truth, I realize how accurate it is. Believing is *work*—it takes energy. It is intentional—it takes time. When I am very busy, sometimes I forget to believe. I don't consciously stop believing, but when I am preoccupied with doing too many other kinds of work, I unconsciously begin to think that I am responsible for the outcome of my work, that I deserve the credit, that God needs me to do this particular job. When I am tired and overextended I find myself praying, "Help me get through this, Lord. Just help me make it." In other words, "Lord, please bless this mess."

When I am in a bless-this-mess way of life, I

have a hard time remembering what it was like to rest in Jesus. I forget that God is my Creator, my Lover. In fact, I begin to act as though I am God—if I don't make something happen, my whole world will suffer. Hanging on for dear life to my own expectations, I let my plans and my schedule overshadow my communion with God and my love for others. And my soul runs dry.

Learning from Jesus
How can we move, then, out of a place of dryness caused by blasphemous busyness into a place of spiritual fruitfulness? The answer to this question is found in what Jesus, as described in Mark's Gospel, did between his busy day and his strange decision to leave Simon's village with so much unfinished. "Very early in the morning, while it was still dark, Jesus got up, left the house and went off to a solitary place, where he prayed" (Mark 1:35). This is not the only place we read about Jesus' going off alone to pray; for example, he went to a mountainside to pray by himself immediately before his famous walk on water (Matthew 14:23-25).

Just as Jesus needed quiet moments of intimacy with his Father, we need to withdraw to quiet places where we can reorient our thinking and discern just what good works God calls us to do, what kind of rest he invites us to experience and what lessons he wants us to learn.

In our busyness, we may settle for the known and familiar ways of doing things, but if we stepped aside more often to pray by ourselves, we might be able occasionally to "walk on water." Only when I sit alone with God, remembering who he is and believing in his unreserved love for me, am I truly ready to go out and serve him. It is in solitude that I reorient my thinking to be sure I am living according to biblical values and not my own misguided intentions. In this solitary place I affirm my desire to follow Jesus and not my world. The prophet Isaiah warned his contemporaries:

> Thus said the Lord GOD, . . .
>   In quietness and trust shall be your strength.
> But you refused, and said,
> "No! We will flee upon horses." (Isaiah 30:15-16 NRSV)

We do the same thing when God invites us to rest in his presence and we say, "No, God, I will not rest, I must ride away on my own plans for my life."

Retreating from everyday life in order to pray is decidedly countercultural. To pull back from my friends, my computer and my job for even a few minutes takes deep determination. Even Jesus had a hard time getting away. His disciples hurried out to find him that morning. "Everyone is looking for you!" they said (Mark 1:36). Likewise, our friends, our computers, our jobs *always* vie for our attention. But if we want to live obedient, faithful lives, we must learn to say no as well as yes, we must be willing to question activities that threaten quietness and trust, and we must listen carefully as the Spirit of God whispers, "This is the way; walk in it" (Isaiah 30:21).

Saying No

Being able to say no requires a tender and humble sensitivity to God. Brennan Manning, in his book *Ruthless Trust*, describes humility this way:

> The heart of humility lies in undivided attention

to God, a fascination with his beauty revealed in creation, a contemplative presence to each person who speaks to us, and a "de-selfing" of our plans, projects, ambitions, and soul. . . . Humble people are without pretense, free from any sense of spiritual superiority, and liberated from the need to be associated with persons of importance. . . . They . . . refuse to take themselves too seriously.[2]

Men and women who are humble enough not to take themselves too seriously are free to say no as well as to say yes. The apostle Paul was humble enough to hear God's no regarding two mission trips. Paul and his companions were "kept by the Holy Spirit from preaching the word in the province of Asia. . . . They tried to go to Bithynia, but the Spirit of Jesus would not allow them to" (Acts 16:6-7). They must have wondered what was going on! Then, through a vision Paul learned that the Holy Spirit wanted them to go to Macedonia.

Twice the Holy Spirit said no. Then the Spirit said yes. The rest, of course, is history—the history of God at work in his people, in his way, in his time.

But how do we determine when it is time to

press on like soldiers (2 Timothy 2:4) and when it is time to quiet our souls "like a child with its mother" (Psalm 131:2)? How do we know whether a request to serve is an opportunity or a temptation? In other words, how do we "test the spirits" (1 John 4:1)?

Paying Attention to God

Jesus said, "Pay attention to how you listen" (Luke 8:18 NRSV). As we listen to Jesus and to God's Word in Scripture, as we listen to our own lives and to the counsel of others, we see signposts that the Holy Spirit uses to guide us on our journey toward peace.

Danger signs. The first signposts we see may read, "Danger! Road closed ahead!" I can think of at least five of these danger signs:

1. If your inner life is seldom joyful, peaceful and ordered, then you are not living in accordance with Scripture.

2. If those close to you (your spouse, your children, those who look to you for emotional and spiritual support) are frequently lonely, discouraged or

disappointed, it may be that you are not available to be used by God in their lives.

3. If considering an activity leaves you feeling emotionally overwhelmed or physically stressed (tightened stomach, extreme fatigue, headaches), God may be using these physical and emotional signs to indicate that a false spirit is prompting you to do something.

4. If you are too busy to pray about an activity, you are too busy to do it.

5. If you are too busy to handle an occasional interruption or emergency, you are too busy.

Have you ever wondered why prison interrupted Paul's ministry? Perhaps God used it to slow Paul down so that he would write letters to the churches. "The human mind plans the way, / but the LORD directs the steps" (Proverbs 16:9). If your schedule is so tight that you cannot meet the unexpected with faith and confidence, then you may be too busy.

The daily examen. Fortunately there are other, more positive signposts to guide us. Ignatius of Loyola (1491-1556), considered by many to be an authority on discernment, taught that we can "test the spirits" by becoming attentive to the "interior movements" of our own hearts. Specifically, we identify God's activity in our lives as we notice our experiences of consolation (peace, joy, confidence) and desolation (anxiety, pain, discouragement).

Ignatius suggested that we do an "examen" (or review) in prayer at the end of each day. Ask what activities or relationships drew you closer to God. Which ones made you feel distant from God? When did you feel most free (a sign of God's presence, according to 2 Corinthians 3:17) and when did you feel least free? What moments were lifegiving and what moments were life-draining? Ignatius taught that by asking these questions daily, we begin to see more clearly how God works in our own lives. Then, when we need to make choices, we will recognize whether activities seem congruent or in conflict with his work in us.

Ignatius brought a perspective to the church that is needed today. Jesus said, "Love the Lord your God with all your heart and with all your soul and with all your mind and with all your strength"

(Mark 12:29). Western culture has emphasized the mind; Ignatius's teaching helps us get in touch with our hearts as well.

Scripture. In addition to the examen, prayerful interaction with Scripture helps us discern which activities are God's custom-made good works for us. Unfortunately, the idea of daily devotions has gotten a bad rap. Some see it as legalistic, others see it as a way to curry God's favor, and still others find Scripture boring.

These problems fade when we think of daily Bible reading as a time for *transformation* rather than for gaining *information*. We can learn much from Scripture, but the deepest longing of our soul is for the Spirit to transform our inner being. This happens as we spend time in quiet with God, absorbing his words and noticing his loving presence.

How we do this varies from person to person. I like a cozy chair and a cup of coffee; others like to share their devotions with a friend. Some like to read through the Bible in a year; others like to think deeply about shorter passages. Many people find that they need the discipline of reading every day, but for others once or twice a week works better. Some pray best when they are walking. I need to be sitting still. Just as all marriage relationships are different from each other, so each person's relationship with God will be unique. The important thing is that we place the highest value on our intimate relationship with our Creator.

Sabbath. Another time to look for signposts in discernment is during a sabbath (Exodus 20:8). Marva Dawn writes that the word *sabbath* means to "cease or desist." This ceasing, she says, is not only from work but

> from the need to accomplish and be productive, from the worry and tension that accompany our modern criterion of efficiency, from our efforts to be in control of our lives as if we were God, from our possessiveness and our enculturation, and finally, from the humdrum and meaninglessness that result when life is pursued without the Lord at the center of it all.[3]

One day each week, as we cease from saying yes to every opportunity, we remind ourselves that

God, in his love, will provide everything we need for life and godliness (2 Peter 1:3).

Letting Go

The daily examen, interaction with Scripture, keeping the sabbath—all of these disciplines remind us that God is God and we are not. This perspective can lead us to a place of *detachment* that allows us to discern more clearly when we should say yes to good works and when we must say no. Detachment from the rewards of human achievement and from the opportunities of technological potential means that we can honestly say to Jesus, "I want to follow your example, and I am committed to embracing your loving desires for my life." This letting go brings us the freedom to hear the divine no as well as the divine yes. It brings us the freedom not to be too busy.

To those of us who are weary and burdened, Jesus says, "Come to me . . . and I will give you rest."

Amen.

Notes

[1] Craig Barnes, *Sacred Thirst: Meeting God in the Desert of Our Longings* (Grand Rapids, Mich.: Zondervan, 2001), pp. 71-72.
[2] Brennan Manning, *Ruthless Trust* (San Francisco: HarperSanFrancisco, 2000), p. 121.
[3] Marva Dawn, *Keeping the Sabbath Wholly* (Grand Rapids, Mich.: Eerdmans, 1989), p. 3.

A former InterVarsity Christian Fellowship staff member, Alice Fryling is currently involved in a ministry of spiritual direction in the Chicago area.